Petitioning for the Impossible
The Prayer of Supplication

D1617244

Petitioning for the Impossible
The Prayer of Supplication

by
Buddy Harrison

Harrison House
Tulsa, Oklahoma

Unless otherwise indicated, all Scripture quotations are taken from the *King James Version* of the Bible.

Petitioning for the Impossible —
The Prayer of Supplication
ISBN 0-89274-900-8
Copyright © 1992 by Buddy Harrison
P. O. Box 35443
Tulsa, Oklahoma 74153

Published by Harrison House, Inc.
P. O. Box 35035
Tulsa, Oklahoma 74153

Printed in the United States of America.

Contents

Acknowledgements

In a man's life there are many acquaintances but few true friends. Because I have several true friends, I am a blessed man. Happy Caldwell and Jerry Savelle are two of my closest friends. They have loved me in spite of myself. For over fifteen years, our three families have taken vacations together and are still friends!

The truths in this book started coming to me as I asked these precious men to pray with me concerning my business affairs. God used both to start me on the road of revelation. I will be eternally grateful to them and expect them to keep me on track concerning continued insights in the Word.

To Happy, thank you for the initial seed planted in my life about the order of prayer. To Jerry, thank you for the additional seed as well as the water which caused those insights to grow and flourish.

I also sincerely appreciate Wayne Mathis for sharing with me the legal side of a petition which makes living the vital side even more enjoyable.

Without these three men and the truth in their lives, I would not be enjoying all that I have now. May the Lord richly bless them.

Petitioning for the Impossible
The Prayer of Supplication

1
Overcoming the Impossible

Have you ever been at a critical point in your life or in a situation that looked almost hopeless? Maybe you even wondered if God could really take what seemed impossible and make it possible.

Well, our God is the God of the impossible, but He also expects us to do our part and pray. There are different types of prayer for different things, and they each have their own guidelines. We must not only know what to pray for and who to pray for, but we must also know how to pray.

That is where the prayer of supplication comes in. It is the kind of prayer that can be used in critical situations where there seems to be no other way. I have used this prayer during times of crisis in my own life, and they have all been answered within three months.

I don't want to make this type of prayer sound like it is going to solve every problem that you have, but when our requests line up with God's will, which is simply His Word, then He hears us and He answers.

One time I found myself in a critical situation when, normally, I would have prayed the prayer of faith or the prayer of agreement to bring the answer. At that time, I learned more about another type of prayer that was even more effective for my particular situation.

The Challenge

It was February of 1989. The Lord had spoken to my wife, Pat, and me to attend Brother Hagin's Winter Seminar.

7

At that time, my publishing company was right in the middle of a new thrust in Bibles called topical Bibles. They were making a strong impact in the Christian market. For us to be able to keep a supply of Bibles available, certain things had to happen.

First of all, my staff told me that we needed a large sum of money to complete this project. We are talking about a six digit figure here! A few days passed, and I wasn't really getting down to serious prayer about it. Finally, the staff told me that I had ten days. Well, then I became serious. I started speeding up saying, "Now Lord, I need the finances to buy Bible paper and leather for the covers."

Eventually, I decided to go to the bank and tell them what I needed. They said they would only loan me a portion of what I had asked for. The problem was not that the bank didn't have the money. They had the money. The problem was they didn't want to give it to me! Having only part of the money wasn't going to cut it. It wouldn't produce what I needed. I needed more than their approved loan. In the natural realm, there was no way.

Not the Prayer of Faith

Usually, I would have depended on Mark 11:24 which says, **What things soever ye desire, when ye pray, believe that ye receive them, and ye shall have them.** But to do that, I needed the inner assurance that when I asked I would receive. And I didn't have it. I guess this gets into that area where you have to know the will of God before you can pray. When you know the will of God in a particular area, then you can also have faith for it. I knew, of course, that it was God's will for all men to be saved and that getting out these topical Bibles would be helping to fulfill His will.

But it was going to take more money than what I had, and seven days had already passed. I still didn't have the inner assurance to pray the prayer of faith. I don't know if you have ever used Mark 11:24 and had nothing happen, but I have. Sometimes you can turn your confessor on overtime. "I believe I receive. I believe I receive. But Lord, it isn't showing up! I believe I receive. I believe I receive." Eventually, you fall into a ritual and don't see any results. Now that wasn't God's fault. It was mine! Well, time was running out, and I knew I had to find another way.

Not the Prayer of Agreement

By now, we were in the middle of the seminar and two of my very close friends, Happy Caldwell and Jerry Savelle, had come to our house and brought their wives. We sat and talked and shared with one another. As we talked, I said to them, "Guys, listen. Pray with me about the money I need for these Bibles. Our first shipment has already sold, and I need to move now to keep Bibles in stock for all the orders we have coming in."

I had three days left when I asked my friends to pray with me. Usually, I would have prayed the prayer of agreement with them using Matthew 18:19 which says, **if two of you shall agree on earth as touching any thing that they shall ask, it shall be done for them of my Father which is in heaven.** But I had recently learned more about the application of the prayer of agreement and knew that the prayer of agreement may not be the most effective prayer to use in this situation.

My insight into the prayer of agreement came to me one day after a service. A young man walked up to me and said, "Brother Harrison, does Matthew 18:19 which says, **if two of you shall agree on earth as touching any thing . . . .** , apply to any thing? Without thinking, it came up out of my spirit, "No." It shocked both of us. I was thinking, "Well, what does it mean then?"

9

My answer was startling to me because I answered him by the Holy Ghost saying, "No, it has to do with any thing *concerning the two of you.* Two people can't agree for Uncle John and Aunt Susy unless their situation also concerns them, but they can intercede *for* them. This, of course, is a different type of prayer." When I saw this, I realized that I could pray the prayer of agreement *with* people but not *for* them. It ended up changing the way I prayed the prayer of agreement.

The Order of Prayer

If I didn't pray the prayer of faith or the prayer of agreement, I wondered exactly how I should pray. After awhile, Happy spoke up and said, "Buddy, in our intercessory group, we have been using the order that is in First Timothy, chapter two, and have been having great success." So, we all turned to First Timothy 2:1 which says, **I exhort therefore, that, first of all, supplications, prayers, intercessions, and giving of thanks, be made for all men.**

As we read, Happy began to tell us what he had found. "We're dealing with four types of prayer here, but they're in an order." When Happy pointed out the order, all of the sudden I realized that God was trying to teach me. How many of you can recognize when God is trying to teach you something? I knew the Holy Ghost was upon him, so I listened closely.

As he was talking, I began to see that there were four kinds of prayer and that they were in a particular order: first supplications, second prayers, third intercessions, and fourth the giving of thanks. Although each of these four types of prayer also work alone, the words, **first of all**, spoke to me of a particular order. God has a certain order that He operates within, and it is my job and your job to understand that order and get in line with it. Unfortunately, many people's prayer lives are out of order, and they simply don't work. But God is a God of order. If you don't understand His order, you mess things up. You need to follow His order so that His blessings can come sweeping into your life.

The Guidelines

I also noticed that all the prayers mentioned in First Timothy, chapter two, were in the plural. In other words, they could be prayed collectively or individually, and they could be prayed multiple times. Some prayers, like the prayer of faith and the prayer of agreement, you pray one time, and that is it. Other prayers, like these, you can pray over and over again.

Some Christians have overemphasized the prayer of faith and the prayer of agreement. Although they are very important and powerful prayers, we have almost forgotten about prayers that can be prayed over and over again. I am not criticizing. I am trying to rectify where we have shoved one type of prayer too far. We have overemphasized the prayer of faith and the prayer of agreement and have been using them when we should have been using other types of prayer.

While Happy continued to teach us what he had found, the Holy Ghost moved on Jerry to say, "We need to pray for the banker and the committee." Then I understood. This prayer in First Timothy, chapter two, was for *men* (people), not money. Why would we pray for people rather than believing for the money? Well, who has the money? The people have the money. God doesn't have any money in heaven. Even if He was to rain money down from heaven, it would be counterfeit, and He isn't a crook. In my situation, the banker was the one who was responsible for the money. He was also the one entrusted with the authority to invest the money.

11

What the Spirit gave to Jerry came alive inside of me, and we began to pray for the banker so that if he had any committees to answer to, we would have favor with them, and if they had any policy that would keep them from giving us the loan, they would be willing to change it in this instance.

The Petition

Then Jerry insisted that we write this prayer out. He said it was because the first word, supplication, meant "petition."[1] If we were going to petition the city, the state or the U. S. government, we would write it out. It would be a formal written request. So we decided to write out our prayer in the form of a legal petition. It ended up being just about one page in length. Every time we made a statement, we wrote a corresponding Scripture reference in the margin. Sometimes we included the references right in the petition.

As we worked together on writing out this petition, we came into closer agreement as to exactly what we were asking. As we searched the Scriptures to find the promises for what we were asking, my faith was being built up, and my spirit man became more and more convinced that what I was asking for was in line with His will for me. After we finished writing it out, we prayed through it. When we finished, I knew in my "knower" that our prayer would be manifested. I just knew that I knew that I knew.

---

[1]James Strong, *The Exhaustive Concordance of the Bible* (McLean: MacDonald Publishing, 1978), "Greek Dictionary of the New Testament," p. 21, #1162.

I was so excited that I called the general manager at my publishing company and said, "Call the bank because they're going to let us have the money." I was excited because I had heard from heaven. I had the witness of the spirit.

The Answer

So the next morning, my general manager called the bank. The first thing the banker said was, "We've reviewed the application again, and we can still only loan you a portion of your request." He waited. Then the banker said, "You know we have never allowed you to borrow money against any of your foreign accounts, author's accounts or C.O.D.'s., but, in this instance, we're going to change our policy." Amen! Our supplication had been answered! By borrowing against our accounts and adding it to the portion that they were willing to loan us, we had the money that was necessary for the topical Bibles.

Since then, I have put into practice what I learned during that week, and I haven't had any major crisis either physically, relationally or financially that couldn't be turned around. I began seeing, in a short amount of time, the answers come to pass for the petitions that I had made. I began to develop a greater hunger for the Word, a stronger love for people and a more intimate relationship with God.

2

Writing the Petition Down

I exhort therefore, that, first of all, supplications, prayers, intercessions, and giving of thanks, be made for all men; For kings, and for all that are in authority; that we may lead a quiet and peaceable life in all godliness and honesty.

For this is good and acceptable in the sight of God our Saviour; Who will have all men to be saved, and to come unto the knowledge of the truth. For there is one God, and one mediator between God and men, the man Christ Jesus; Who gave himself a ransom for all, to be testified in due time.

1 Timothy 2:1-6

The first kind of prayer mentioned in this passage is the prayer of supplication. It is one of the most powerful prayers in the Word of God because it is so specific and exact. Some prayers are general, so you get general answers. The prayer of supplication is specific, so you get specific answers. In this type of prayer, you can't just go by inspiration. You must take time out to put it in writing. If you can't write out your request, it still isn't real to you. A vision doesn't really become real to you unless you have it written down. Habakkuk admonishes us to write the vision down and make it plain so they that read it may run with it. (Hab. 2:2.) Sometimes, we lose in the kingdom of God simply because we haven't taken the time to write things down. But when we do, we will be able to overcome what seemed to us to be impossible.

I have also found that the progression in prayer that First Timothy 2:1 seems to suggest has helped to bring me to the place that I know that my prayers are answered when I ask. When I am having difficulty discerning the will of God in a matter, when my faith seems low and I don't have the inner assurance, or when I need others to pray in one accord with me about a situation that seems impossible, I find myself using the prayer of supplication.

There are actually three definitions for the word supplication: 1) a petition, 2) an entreaty or 3) a humble request.[1]

A Petition

The primary definition for supplications in this verse is "petition" according to *Strongs*.[2] A petition is a "formal written request."[3] It is written in formal terms that deal with the legal side of an issue. It follows acceptable, proper, legal guidelines and is addressed to a person or group in authority. It also requires that some judicial action be taken.

In First Timothy 2:1, the Greek word for *supplications* is *deesis*. In the New Testament, this supplication is "always addressed to God" as He is the Supreme Authority.[4]

---

[1]*Webster's New Twentieth Century Dictionary*, 2nd ed., s.v. "supplication."
[2]Strong, p. 21, #1162.
A *petition* is a "formal written request."[3]
[3]*Webster's*, s.v. "petition."
[4]W.E. Vine, *An Expository Dictionary of New Testament Words* (Old Tappan: Fleming H. Revell, 1966), p. 200.

An Entreaty

An *entreaty* is "an earnest request." When a request is earnest, it is "1) serious and intense; not joking or playful; zealous and sincere; deeply convinced, 2) intent; fixed, and 3) serious; important; not trivial."[5]

This is a time when you get down to business and are determined. There is an intensity present. The Greek word for supplication used here, *deesis*, "stresses the sense of need" rather than just desire or want.[6]

Too much prayer is passive. It is just fellowship, just communion with God. But when we are talking about a supplication, it is intense.

James 5:16 talks about the effectual fervent prayer of the righteous man and says that it avails much. Jesus, speaking about the days of John the Baptist until now, says, **the kingdom of heaven suffereth violence, and the violent take it by force** (Matt. 11:12). Some things won't ever get done until you get violent with them. You must make up your mind that you need to have them and that it has to be that way.

There are privileges in being bold that many people don't understand. We need to see that God tells us that He wants us to **come boldly unto the throne of grace, that we may obtain mercy, and find grace to help in time of need** (Heb. 4:16). Too many people don't know the will of God; therefore, when it is time to pray, they come playing games. God wants you to come seriously, knowing what His Word says and what you need. He wants you to come boldly.

---

[5]*Webster's*, s.v. "earnest."
[6]Vine, p. 200.

People who are desperate and in need don't say, "Well, God, if you think it would be all right." When your back is against the wall and you are facing a life or death situation and your whole future is at stake, you need to be exact and bold. You need to walk in and say to the Lord, "You said in your Word it's this way, this way and this way, and I'm not going to have it any other way." That is not getting smart with God. That is putting Him in remembrance of His Word. (Isa. 43:26.)

A Humble Request

Just because a person is bold doesn't mean that he is proud. A person can be bold but humble at the same time. James 4:6 says, **God resisteth the proud, but giveth grace unto the humble.** In just the next breath, James commands us to submit ourselves to God. (James 4:7.) And that is exactly what one meaning of the word humble is — "submissive to the divine will."[7] Submissive to who? To God and to His Word. In other words, your request must be submitted to God and to His Word. It must be humble. It can't go contrary to His Word because then you would be out of His will.

Oftentimes the struggle in prayer has to do with accepting the will of God. In Luke 22:44, Jesus was in agony and **prayed more earnestly: and his sweat was as it were great drops of blood falling down to the ground.** Jesus, in the garden, was in agony and was struggling with the will of God for His life. Some things that you pray about and deal with can be so hard that a struggle goes on between the spiritual and the natural. Jesus prayed until the will of His soul was conformed to the will of His Father. He prayed

---

[7]*Webster's,* s.v. "humble."

until He could come to that place where He could say
. . . not my will, but thine, be done (Luke 22:42). At that
point, His mind, will and emotions were brought into
subjection to the will of God. We, like Jesus, need to pray
until our will is in line with God's will, for only then can
we be assured that He will answer.

According to James 4:3, **Ye ask, and receive not, because
ye ask amiss, that ye may consume it upon your lusts.** But
when you humble yourself by submitting your will to His
will, your prayers will come to pass because you will be
praying His will. Because you have submitted your will to
His will, your soul will prosper. Your emotions will be under
His control. Your mind can be selective in its thought
processes, and you can make better choices because they
will be made according to the Word of God.

Supplications in Paul's Letters

Nearly every letter that Paul wrote included his prayers
for that church. Although many times he was dealing with
situations in the church, he was also telling them how he
was praying for them. That is how he affected them with
his letters. He wrote down the supplication that he was
praying for them.

In Ephesians 1:16-19, he ceases not to give thanks for
them, making mention of them in his prayers. He asks that
the Lord give them the spirit of wisdom and revelation in
the knowledge of Him, that the eyes of their understanding
be enlightened, that they would know the hope of his calling,
the riches of the glory of his inheritance and the exceeding
greatness of his power.

In Ephesians 3:14-19, he bows his knees asking the Lord
to strengthen them with might by His Spirit so that Christ
can dwell in their hearts by faith, they can be rooted and

grounded in love and be able to comprehend and know the love of Christ. The outcome he asks for is that they be filled with the fullness of God.

In Philippians 1:9-11, he prays that their love will abound in knowledge and judgement so that they will approve things that are excellent and be sincere and without offence till the day of Christ.

In Colossians 1:9-13, he prays that they be filled with the knowledge of his will so they can walk worthy of the Lord, be fruitful in every good work, increase in the knowledge of God and be strengthened with all might while they are giving thanks to the Father for making them meet to be partakers of the inheritance, delivering them from the power of darkness and translating them into the kingdom.

In Romans 15:30, he says, . . . **strive together with me in your prayers to God for me.** In this verse, he is asking the churches to join him in prayer. The key phrase here is *strive together* which means "to struggle in the company with."[8] Literally, this word means "to compete for a prize." In a figurative sense, it means "to contend with an adversary."[9] Because Paul wrote down his prayer, the church was able to strive together with him in prayer more closely. They could come into agreement to a greater degree and be more certain that they were in one accord. United prayers of this kind can be very powerful. Acts 4:31 records an instance where the place which the believers were standing on shook after they had prayed in one accord.

---

[8]Strong, p.68, #4865.
[9]Strong, p. 8, #75.

Notice also that Paul was not too proud to ask the church to pray for him. Sometimes we as ministers need to follow Paul's example and recognize that we too have needs. We too can be helped by the body of Christ as much as they can be helped by us. All we have to do is humble ourselves and ask.

These are just a few of the prayers that he prayed for the churches he was overseeing. In every instance, he had addressed his request for them to God and had taken the time to write it out in his letter. I had never noticed that until I started doing some research.

Supplications in David's Psalms

While the supplications in the Epistles deal with the present-day Church and the will of God for our generation, the Psalms also contain a number of supplications. One supplication that David makes can be found in Psalm 119:170 where he says, **Let my supplication come before thee: deliver me according to thy word.**

How does God deliver? He delivers according to His Word. What is your supplication based on? Is it based on His Word? If so, that is where the power is.

In Psalm 28:2, David says, **Hear the voice of my supplications, when I cry unto thee . . . .** In verse 6, he says, **Blessed be the Lord, because he hath heard the voice of my supplications.** In verse 7, he says, **The Lord is my strength and my shield; my heart trusted in him, and I am helped . . . .** That sounds like answered prayer to me. It sounds like David was getting somewhere. It was working for him and blessing him.

There is always an assurance of Him hearing and answering all our petitions. Why? Because they are all based on the will of God, which is His Word. Psalm 30:8-12 says, **I cried to thee, O Lord; and unto the Lord I made supplication. . . . Thou hast turned for me my mourning into dancing: thou hast put off my sackcloth, and girded me with gladness; To the end that my glory may sing praise to thee, and not be silent.** God heard David's supplication, and He answered. God will hear your supplication, and He will answer. He is wanting to work in your behalf.

Property Sells

Once I began to see what the Scriptures were saying about writing down my requests, I began to teach my staff about it. At that time, the ministry owned a beautiful piece of property on top of a mountain. It had ten wooded acres with two bluffs that dropped two hundred feet into a lake. It was beautiful and scenic.

Now the Lord was telling me to sell the property because He planned to use it for ministers, and He wanted us to have property within an hours drive from the office. This property was five hours away.

So the staff and I petitioned the Lord about selling the property. I received in my spirit the amount that we should ask for the property. One week later, we had a contract in our hands for $5,000 more than the amount I had had in my spirit. We paid a $5,000 fee to the person who sold it for us, and we received the amount I knew the Lord had told me to expect.

A Company Rehires

Not only did I begin teaching my staff to write down their petitions, I also began teaching it to the people in churches across the nation. One time I preached this in a church in Tucson. An engineer there went to work the next day and was laid off from the company he was in.

As he was putting up his things, he came across his Bible, and the thought hit him that he ought to present a supplication like Brother Harrison had taught. He took out his Bible, sat down at his desk, searched the Scriptures and wrote out his petition. Thirty minutes later, but before he had left the building, a man from another division of the company walked in and hired him at more money than he had been making! Losing your job can be critical. God didn't want him doing without, and he didn't have to do without. Instead, he received an increase.

A New Company Starts

Another man, in the same church, owned a dental supply business. He had tried to put together a new company in Phoenix, but nothing came of it. He tried to get investors to put a package together, and nothing happened. After I taught this on Sunday, he went home and wrote out his petition then prayed.

On Wednesday, he received a certified letter in the mail. The financier that was backing him said he wanted to open a company in Phoenix. The letter stated that they would do it only under certain conditions: 1) if he was the president and C.E.O., 2) if he made a certain amount of money and 3) if he kept his own company. The conditions met his needs exactly, so, with the backing of the financier, he started a company. Now he is on his way to becoming a millionaire.

An Unfaithful Husband Returns

One woman had been receiving phone calls from another woman telling her that her husband was unfaithful to her. She had seen some signs that what the woman was telling her may have been true, but she didn't want to believe it. She didn't know exactly how to handle the situation and decided to write out a supplication. Her supplication was one of protection as she asked that any influences or people that would affect her husband in an adverse way be removed from his life. In just a short period of time, her husband's attitude changed, and their relationship became so good and so strong that she was thoroughly confident that he wouldn't be bothered anymore.

A Special Education Program Accepts a Child

Another woman was trying to get her child accepted into a special education program that she felt he needed to have. They didn't want to accept him because they felt like he wasn't quite severe enough, yet he really wasn't receiving the help he needed at a regular school. After talking with them and hearing me teach, she went back and began to write a supplication addressing her situation. In just a couple of weeks, they contacted her and said, ''Well, we do have an opening, so we'll go ahead and take him.''

A House Sells

I also taught this message to our ministers in Delaware where a young lady and her husband had been trying to buy a house for two months. They couldn't get anywhere with all that would keep coming up about property financing. She had been hassling with this for months. After the service, they took out the Scriptures, wrote out their supplication then prayed. The next day at 3:00 p.m., the people called and said, ''We don't understand it, but the board decided to approve your loan. You have your loan and your house.'' They moved in within two weeks time and have been there ever since.

3
Backing the Petition Up

In supplications, you are dealing with the known will of God. If you don't know His will, you are in trouble because you can't change the known will of God. The known will of God is written in His Word. If you will allow the Holy Ghost to lead you and bring to your remembrance Scriptures, you will be writing under the anointing and unction of the Holy Ghost and of God as you write out your petition and the Scriptures to back it up. If it is in agreement with His Word, you can be sure that it is a part of His will for you.

His Word Is His Will

In Isaiah 43:26, God said, **Put me in remembrance: let us plead together: declare thou, that thou mayest be justified.** Why? Because His Word is His will. When somebody writes out his or her will, they are writing out a legal document. Your Bible is a legal document. It is a testimony to what His will is.

Whenever someone dies, an executor is assigned to carry out the will. He is responsible for reinforcing it and making sure that the instructions are followed. Jesus died to make sure God's will would come to pass, and He rose up to watch over it and make sure that it did! He is watching over it to make it good. He is enforcing His own will. Whatever is in that legal document is ours. We have new

25

life. We are new creations. Old things have passed away, and all things have become new. (2 Cor. 5:17.) We are the head and not the tail. We are above and not beneath. (Deut. 28:13.) All of the blessings of God are legally ours.

The Legal Side and the Vital Side

But if you don't know what rightfully belongs to you according to the Word of God, how will you ever be able to experience all that God has provided for you? Your petition establishes, in you and those who may be petitioning with you, the known will of God. This is the legal side of the petition. Once it is established in you, you are in line to experience the will of God in your life. This is the vital side, the practical living side. But before the vital side can be experienced, the legal side must first be established. If it happens any other way, you can just chalk it up to God's mercy and grace operating in your behalf.

Take, for example, the purchase of a house. If you buy a house, you can't enjoy living in it until you have legally completed all the paperwork and actually paid for it. There is the legal side of having a house, and there is the vital side, where you actually live in the house. So it is with the promises of God. Legally, God's promises are bought, purchased and paid for, but then there is the vital side, where you actually get a chance to experience His promises in your life. In the church world, we are trying to deal with the vital side when we don't yet even understand the legal side.

The Supreme Court of Heaven

In a court case, you deal with facts, evidence and proof. The facts of God's Word make the difference. What about the evidence? Your faith is your evidence. **Now faith is the**

substance of things hoped for, the evidence of things not seen (Heb. 11:1). The Word of God becomes proof to you and to the enemy that you have what you are believing for.

In a supplication, you are dealing with the known will of God, which is the Word of God, and you are appealing to the Supreme Court of heaven. Now, Satan is the head of his kingdom. (2 Cor. 4:4.) He has wicked spirits in high places. He has rulers of the darkness, powers and principalities. (Eph. 6:12.) He is the accuser of the brethren. (Rev. 12:10.) If you get out of line in one spot, he is there to condemn you. If you make one mistake, he will legally take advantage of you. He is a legalist.

But thanks be to God. God is not a legalist. When you miss it, He is there to restore you. Lamentations 3:22,23 promises that **. . . his compassions fail not. They are new every morning: great is thy faithfulness.** God is working for you, not against you. Besides that, He is the Supreme Judge of the universe. When you make your appeal to Him, you are going to the Supreme Court of heaven. When you bring your supplication, you are walking into the court of heaven where God is the Most High God. There isn't anybody any higher than He is. When you use His Word in His court, you win! When you know that, you are bold. It is not hit and miss. There is a way to pray in absolute confidence so that there are no questions, no doubts that you have the answer.

You have an Advocate. His name is Jesus. (1 John 2:1.) He is the Lawyer Who pleads your case. How? Whatever words that you say to Him are what He uses to plead your case. So if you use His words to plead your case in His Father's court, the outcome is sure. The case is fixed!

Then, of course, you have the Holy Ghost Who is the Sheriff. A judge can decree a thing and pass judgement on it, but there must be an enforcer, someone who will enforce that word. That is the Holy Ghost. He makes sure God's Word is carried out down here. The angels do their part also.

A Petition of the First Century Church

In Acts, chapter four, Peter and John were preaching to the people, and the priests seized them and put them in prison overnight. When the priests released them the next day, they returned to their own company and told them what had happened.

After they told them, everyone **lifted up their voice to God with one accord** (Acts 4:24). How do you get in one accord? You say the same thing. One sure way to get everyone to say the same thing is to write down the request. It seems that even the early church must have written down their request. How do I know they wrote it down? It is written in the Scripture, isn't it?

Their request seems to follow the form of a petition. They begin in Acts 4:24 by listing the Scriptures relative to their situation. First, they go to Genesis and magnify the God of all creation. They remind Him and themselves that He created the heaven, the earth, the sea and all that are in them.

Then they go to the Psalms and quote the words of David from Psalm 2:1,2 which speak of the rejection of the Messiah and His anointed.

In verses 26 and 27, they identify four classes of people that came against Christ: the kings of the earth, the rulers of Israel, the heathen Gentiles, and the people of Israel. In verse 29, they ask the Lord to behold the threats that are being hurled against them by these same people.

After identifying the Scriptures that applied to their situation, they make their request and ask for boldness to speak His Word and for signs and wonders to be done by the name of Jesus.

Their request was in line with God's will which is to go into all the world and preach the gospel to every creature. (Mark 16:15.) They had completed the legal side of their request. Now they were ready to experience the vital side.

Well, they don't have to wait long because in verse 31, their first request is answered when the place where they are standing is shaken, and they are all filled with the Holy Ghost and begin to speak the Word with boldness. Their second request is answered shortly thereafter when they hit the streets. Acts 5:12 records that many signs and wonders were wrought among the people by the hands of the apostles.

Was the supplication answered? Yes, one part was answered instantly and the other later. God is always ready to answer your supplications because God lives in the eternal now. God is the great I am. (Ex. 3:14.) *Am* is in the present tense. He is ready to do it now, so when you pray, believe that the promises of God are yea and amen in Christ Jesus. (2 Cor. 1:20.)

A Personal Petition

Now write down your own petition to God. You can't copy another person's supplication. You have to get in the Word of God and write your own. You need to know why you said what you said, and it needs to be real to you. The Holy Ghost will lead and guide you into all truth. As you pray in the Holy Spirit, He will begin to lead you to Scriptures. You may also want to thumb through the Epistles, Psalms and Proverbs. As you read the Word of God and study, you will find Scriptures that you know will fit in your petition. Mark and write them down, so you will have them to refer to when you begin.

The only caution that I might add is that you not include in your petition any dates. I did this a couple of times and hadn't received an answer to them for quite a few months. My spirit stayed slightly grieved, but I couldn't understand why. The Lord said, ''Go back and look at your petitions.'' So I went back and looked, and He said, ''You know why they weren't answered and why you were frustrated in your spirit? It was because you wrote dates in it. You can have goals without dates.'' I was reminded then of Mark 11:24 which says, **What things soever ye desire,** *when ye pray,* *believe that ye receive* **them, and ye shall have them.** The emphasis here is on believing that you receive *when you pray.* Except for those two petitions that I added dates to, they have all been answered within one to ninety days.

As you are writing out your petition, you may want to refer to the one that I wrote below. Write yours out however works best for you. In the appendix, I have also included a more technical petition written by a Christian attorney, Wayne Mathis. You may also want to refer to his petition when you are writing your own.

Petitioner's Original Request

Eph. 6:17,18	This petition is being brought to God because of His Word. It is being
Rom. 13:1	brought to the Highest Authority in the universe over the supreme court.
1 John 2:2	I am represented by Jesus Christ, my Advocate. There has been a change of
Col. 1:13	representation by counsel, and Satan no longer represents me because he is not my lord or lawyer any longer.
Ps. 100:4	I am thankful that I can petition this
Ps. 116:1,2	court, for God has done great things
Ps. 136	for me. My account has been identified

Ps. 118:1-6	by the written Word, and again I want
Ps. 105:5-8	to give thanks. All relief for petitioners
Ps. 18:1-6	was granted in full.

The basis for grant of relief in contract is established by the Old Covenant with Abraham, because

Heb. 6:13 — He could swear by no greater, He sware by Himself. But I have a

Heb. 8:6 — better covenant established upon

Gal. 3:29 — better promises. I became an heir,

Gal. 3:13,14 — through my Agent, Jesus, when He

Col. 2:13,14 — sealed it by His blood for a new

Heb. 9:15 — covenant.

Write in the verses that apply to your specific requests in the column below.

Therefore, I have every right to be here and have the relief sought, and You, God, have the authority to issue a decree in this matter.
So I request to be granted the following specific request for relief:

_____ 1. _____

_____

_____ 2. _____

_____

_____ 3. _____

_____

John 10:10 — For Satan has come as a thief to steal, to kill and to destroy, but Your

Ps. 119:170 — promise to me was in Your Word and by Your Spirit which You gave me.

Ps. 4:6-8
1 John 5:14,15

This is the petitioner's prayer, and I am asking for a summary judgement. I cast all of my care on You, for I know You have heard me, and I have it.

So therefore, it is ordered, adjudged and decreed that the petitioner receive that relief sought in this petition immediately according to Mark 11:23,24.

Ps. 103:20

Be it further ordered, adjudged and decreed that the agents of God implement such findings immediately pursuant to the Word. In other words, Holy Ghost and angels do God's Word.

Again, let me say thank you for all you have done and are doing now. I know you shall continue to bless all who seek and serve you.

DATED THIS THE_____ DAY OF_____, 19____.

PETITIONERS:

_____   _____
(name)   (name)

_____   _____
(name)   (name)

_____   _____
(name)   (name)

ANSWERED THIS THE_____ DAY OF_____, 19____.

Establishing the Known Will of God

This petition is simply a pattern to declare your rights and privileges. When you write out your petitions based upon the Word of God, you are establishing the known will of God. Then when you pray it aloud, you are building up your faith in what you already know, for **faith cometh by hearing, and hearing by the word of God** (Rom. 10:17). Faith is essential to prayer, for faith is the recognition of, and the committal of yourself and your matters to, the faithfulness of God. Becoming established in the known will of God helps you to ask in faith with nothing wavering so that you can receive from the Lord what He has already promised you. (James 1:5-8.)

When you pray your petition, you should pray it as a present possession, as if you already possessed it. Hebrews 11:1 says that faith is in the now, not in the past or the future. It is in the now. It is in the present. There is a certainty to it. If time passes and the petition that you made starts to ebb away from you, and you don't feel like you have it, go back and read it again until it gets down on the inside of you so that you know that you know that you know. For **without faith it is impossible to please him** (Heb. 11:6).

4

Praying the Petition Through

The Word says in First John 5:14,15, . . . **if we ask any thing according to his will, he heareth us: And if we know that he hear us, whatsoever we ask, we know that we have the petitions that we desired of Him.** According to this verse, we must first *ask* according to His will, and secondly, we must *know* that He hears us.

The prayer of supplication, since it is based on the Word of God, helps us to pray according to the will of God. It has always caused me to search the Scriptures so that when I pray I am literally praying the Word of God.

The Word of God Praying

Both the Word of God and prayer are mentioned when Paul talks to the church in Ephesus about spiritual warfare. In Ephesians, chapter six, Paul expounds on the armor of God:

> **Wherefore take unto you the whole armour of God, that ye may be able to withstand in the evil day, and having done all, to stand. Stand therefore, having your loins girt about with truth, and having on the breastplate of righteousness; And your feet shod with the preparation of the gospel of peace;**

> **Above all, taking the shield of faith, wherewith ye shall be able to quench all the fiery darts of the wicked. And take the helmet of salvation, and the sword of the Spirit, which is the word of God: Praying always with all prayer and supplication in the Spirit,**

**and watching thereunto with all perseverance and
supplication for all saints.**

Ephesians 6:13-18

When Paul lists the armor, he talks about two kinds
of armor — the defensive and the offensive. Notice that the
Word of God and prayer are the only two pieces of the
armor that are offensive while all the other pieces are
defensive. It is when we are on the offensive with the enemy
that we can do more than hold our ground. When we take
an offensive position, we can actually claim what rightfully
belongs to us. That is what the prayer of supplication does.

Most of the time, we think about the sword of the Spirit,
that he mentions, as being in our hand, but the sword of
the Spirit is really in our mouths. When Paul was writing
to the church, he was writing a letter. When you write a
letter, you don't break it up and number it. The numbers
were added to Paul's letter so we could reference what he
said and refer to them for study purposes, but the original
letters weren't divided up.

So if we read Ephesians 6:17,18, forgetting the
punctuation and the numbering in an effort to bring back
the original flow of the language, it would read, **Take the
helmet of salvation and the sword of the Spirit which is
the word of God praying.** This reading emphasizes that the
sword of the Spirit is the **word of God praying.** Jesus is
the Word. Jesus knows how to pray, and He is powerful.

If, in turn, I am using the equipment that God has given
me, the Word of God praying, His words become my
words. I am taking His Word and praying His Word. Isaiah
55:11 says, **So shall my word be that goeth forth out of my
mouth: it shall not return unto me void, but it shall
accomplish that which I please, and it shall prosper in the
thing whereto I sent it.**

Notice also that it is **the word of God praying always
with all prayer** (Eph. 6:18). The Amplified translation of this

verse says, **with all [manner of] prayer.** Where we have made a mistake much of the time is that we have come along and have used the wrong prayer in the wrong situation. We pray the wrong prayer and wonder why we don't get results. We have just lacked knowledge in some areas, and God wants to expand our knowledge because knowledge is a vital part in living the victorious life.

Going further in verse 18, Paul says, **Praying always with all prayer and supplication in the Spirit, and watching thereunto with all perseverance and supplication for all saints.** He mentions a specific type of prayer here — supplication. But notice, it is supplication *in the Spirit for all saints.* We should be praying for our brothers and sisters in the Lord and praying for one another.

Why? Because it is a part of the armor of God. The armor is more than just praying in the Holy Ghost. It is also praying the Word of God. It is literally Jesus' Word being prayed out.

What do you have? You have the sword of the Spirit which is coming out of your mouth which is the Word of God praying. What makes it so powerful and dynamic? Why is it God can't refuse to answer this supplication? Why will it always be answered? Because you are praying the Word of God which is full of life and eternal. (Isa. 40:8.) You are praying His own Word. For Him to deny His Word, He has to deny Himself. God can't deny Himself. (2 Tim. 2:13.) He is Who He is, and His Word has said so. Therefore, bless God, it shall be so. It is not a hope so or a maybe so. It is a fact. It is a certainty.

Prayed More Than Once

A supplication can be prayed more than once. Every time the situation seems like it isn't lining up with my petition, I get the supplication out and pray it again. This produces faith in me. It brings me an assurance; therefore, I am not unstable or wavering. I pray it until I am established in it. Sooner or later, it has to come to pass. Most of the time, it is sooner rather than later.

The church, when they were praying for Peter's release from prison in Acts 12:5-17, prayed without ceasing. Peter was to die. (Acts 12:1-4.) The church was praying for him, using the armor of God. The church began praying in the morning and continued on into the night. God was at work, but they didn't know it yet.

Verse 5 says, **Peter therefore was kept in prison: but prayer was made without ceasing of the church unto God for him.** *Without ceasing* literally means "stretched out" which "signifies earnest, fervent."[1]

You know what a person or animal looks like when running a race? They are stretched out intensely the closer that they get to the finish line. They are earnestly and fervently trying to make it over to the other side.

In supplications in the Spirit, the Holy Ghost begins to take over. Even though you may not be praying in tongues, you will be praying by the aid of the Spirit of God, by the power of the Spirit of God. (Rom. 8:26,27.) You will find yourself stretching out to grab it, take hold of it and lock on to it.

So the church is down to serious business because Peter is in trouble. This isn't a passive prayer. This is an active prayer. This is a prayer that brings supernatural deliverance to Peter while he is still in chains. That very night while Peter is sleeping, an angel of the Lord comes to him in the prison and smotes him on the side saying . . . **Arise up quickly** (Acts 12:7). The chains fall off from Peter's hands,

---

[1]Vine, p. 177.

and he follows the angel out of the prison, through the gate and out onto the streets. Soon after, the angel departs from him, and he runs back to the group that had been praying for him without ceasing. Their instant and earnest supplication for him throughout the night had literally saved his life.

So, the church had made their request according to His will. They had met the first condition mentioned in First John 5:14,15. But they also met the second condition, which is to know that He hears us. They continued in prayer until they knew that they knew.

I have found that the progression in prayer that First Timothy 2:1 seems to suggest has helped to bring me to that place of knowing. Once I know, nothing and nobody can stop me from receiving the petitions that I desire of Him. His Word and the witness of His Spirit with my spirit make me certain it is already mine, and He won't deny His Word.

Prayers

The second kind of prayer mentioned in First Timothy, chapter two, is often linked with supplication in other passages of Scripture (Acts 1:14; Eph. 6:18; Phil. 4:6; 1 Tim. 5:5.) *Prayers,* in First Timothy 2:1, means "worship."[2]

Worship is actually a form of prayer. I am not talking here about mental or physical worship. I am talking about spiritual worship.

In John 4:24, it says, **God is a Spirit: and they that worship him must worship him in spirit and in truth.** You, as a spirit being, worship a Spirit Being, so everything has to begin at that point. The raising of hands, for example, may be worship, and it may not. If you are thinking about

---

[2]Strong, p. 61, #4335.

the roast you have cooking in the oven at home for dinner and are wondering if it will burn or if all you are thinking about is eating that roast, that is not worship. You are just raising your hands. But if you are focusing on God as the object of your worship and are becoming more and more conscious of Him while you are raising your hands, then you are really worshipping.

Because you are a spirit being and because you are filled with the Holy Spirit, He helps you in your worship. Your spirit is the part of you that motivates you to worship. Your mind and your body simply respond to or fall in line with your spirit.

See, you start out with supplications which deal with the known will of God. You are using your mind when you write down your supplication because it has to do with what you know. Then you begin to worship. Why is that? Worship is the link, or hookup, that takes you from the mental realm into the spiritual realm so you can get into intercession. In other words, you are moving from one dimension into another. You are moving out of the natural, logical, mental realm and into the spiritual realm as you begin to worship.

First, you worship with your understanding, then, as the Spirit leads you, you worship using the language of the spirit, which is tongues. One is in a known language while the other is in an unknown language.

Intercessions

As you begin to worship or pray in an unknown language or tongue, the Holy Ghost will begin to take over and intercede through you for the things you don't know about. According to Paul in Romans, **. . . we know not what we should pray for as we ought: but the Spirit itself maketh intercession for us with groanings which cannot be uttered** (Rom. 8:26). The Spirit Paul is talking about here is the Holy

40

Spirit. Jesus referred to Him as **another Comforter** in John 14:16.

Comforter in the Greek literally means "called to one's side." Historically, the word *comforter* "was used in a court of justice to denote a legal assistant, counsel for the defence, an advocate; then, generally, one who pleads another's cause, an intercessor, advocate."[3] The word **another** here implies that they are of the same sort rather than a different sort. In other words, the Holy Ghost and Jesus are made of the same stuff, and they are working together along side us in the heavenly court of justice.

At some point while I am praying in tongues, the Holy Ghost begins to take over. He begins to intercede through me. The word, *intercessions*, as it is used in First Timothy 2:1, means "seeking the presence and hearing of God on behalf of others." At one time, it was "a technical term for approaching a king, and so for approaching God in intercession."[4]

In other words, the Holy Ghost is coming along side of you and helping you to pray. Because He is apart of the Godhead, He knows all things and is able to pray for things that you don't even know about. He also will not pray anything that would be against the will of God. He can only pray the will of God. So when you finish, you know that you have prayed the perfect prayer and have covered all the bases.

---

[3]Vine, p. 208.
[4]Vine, p. 267.

Whenever I get through interceding, I know that I know. If I don't get to that place, I get quiet and go back and worship God again. Usually, I receive an utterance in tongues and interpret it. Through the interpretation, God tells me what I have to do next so that I am never in the dark. I either know I have it, or I know what to do next. It gets rid of those "well let's pray and leave it up to God" prayers. In First Corinthians 14:15, Paul mentions a similar approach, **I will pray with the spirit, and I will pray with the understanding also: I will sing with the spirit, and I will sing with the understanding also.** By beginning with supplications then moving into worship and intercessions, prayer is taken out of the mystical realm and put into the spiritual order of God so that it can work.

Giving of Thanks

Following the prayer of supplication, spiritual worship, and intercession is, what should be, a very natural response — the giving of thanks. In the giving of thanks, we express gratitude. Surely if we ask someone for something and they promise to give it to us, plain old common courtesy would say, "Thank you." When you ask God for something He has promised you in His Word, you shouldn't have to be told to say, "Thank you." Yet many petitions are not complete simply because they lack a word of thanks.

Today, we live in an instant society, and we want to approach God on that instant basis. Then we wonder why it isn't working too well. Anything worthwhile takes time. If you are going to have a good marriage, it is going to take time. If you are going to have a good church, it is going to take time.

You might say, "But God, I asked you. How come I don't have it?" First of all, you may have a bad attitude. You may not have a thankful heart. You need to be kind and gracious. He saved you. He healed you. He filled you with His Spirit. You have so many things to be thankful for.

Sometimes, when just one little thing goes wrong, you get all uptight. You go to Him in prayer, and He turns your whole life around, but you don't even take the time out to say, ''Thank You.'' Maybe all you need to do is remember to thank Him for the many things He has already done for you and for all that you know He is going to do. Those two words, as small as they are, can make all the difference.

David Prospers

Psalm 118:1-29 is a biblical example of what I call the sandwich theory, which places the request in the middle of the prayer and thanksgiving at the beginning and the end. David spends the first twenty-four verses of his petition giving thanks to God because: He is good, His mercy endures forever, He answers when David calls on Him, He puts him in a large place, He is on David's side, He takes his part, He is his strength, song, and salvation, and finally just because He has heard him. It is interesting to notice here that his petition is only one verse long: **Save now, I beseech thee, O Lord: O Lord, I beseech thee, send now prosperity** (v. 24). Then after he has made his request, he goes back to thanking and praising God in the last four verses. Was his petition answered? Well, who was only a shepherd boy and became the king of Israel? Who defeated the enemy battle after battle and walked away with the spoils? David did, and God helped him! He was a man after God's own heart who prospered. David was more conscious of giving thanks unto God than of his need.

Ten Lepers Healed

In the story of the ten lepers, found in Luke 17:12-19, all the lepers were healed and cleansed but only one was made whole. He was a Samaritan, not a Jew. He had returned to thank and praise Jesus for what He had done. Jesus told him that his faith had made him whole.

The skin of lepers often rotted off. Many times, they would lose members of their body. All ten were healed and cleansed, but the leper who returned to thank and praise Him also had his members restored. God will honor faith, and healing will come. But if you have an attitude of gratitude, you will be made whole. That which is missing will be replaced.

People who are looking for miracles need to write a supplication. Why? Because when you write a supplication with the right attitude and thank God, you will get your answer. You will spend more time on the thank you than on the request. Isn't it easy to say thank you when He has done such great things?

A Good Deal

For some time, I had been wanting my son to be able to get a different car. He had a sports car. Living in an apartment and endeavoring to go to school, he couldn't handle the more expensive car. What he needed was a more economical car, but you know how twenty-year-olds are. The car has to look good. The economical part isn't so important. What he needed was a car that was economical *and* looked good.

So, I petitioned the Lord concerning a car for him. I listed all that was important to my son and to me. I petitioned the Lord on Saturday. On the way home after church Sunday night, I bought a newspaper. I went through the paper marking the cars that looked interesting to me.

I got up praying the next morning, praising and thanking God for Him leading me to do the right thing. My eyes were drawn to one particular car, so I called the owner.

The car sounded like it would be a good deal. I drove out and saw it. It looked good. I called my son and had him meet me. He saw it and liked it. By 11:00 a.m., we had found and bought a car, and you know how long that can sometimes take! All we had to do was let our request be made known to God and begin thanking Him for it.

For Those in Authority

The verses following First Timothy 2:1 tell you exactly who you should pray for, **For kings, and for all that are in authority.** You may have a tendency to take this verse of Scripture and pray for the president. I know I did. Why? We thought we were praying for those in authority, so we prayed for the king, prime minister, judges, supreme court or someone in a high position. But look again at verses 1 and 2. He says, **I exhort therefore, that, first of all, supplications, prayers, intercessions, and giving of thanks, be made for all men; For kings, and for all that are in authority.** The first verse emphasizes, **for all men,** while the second verse says, **for kings.** Do you realize that God has made all believers kings according to Revelations 1:6? In other words, this Scripture also applies to the believer. Ephesians 6:18 also emphasizes the believer when referring to prayer and supplication. The only difference is that this verse uses the phrase . . . **for all saints.**

The second part of verse 2 says, **for all that are in authority.** According to W. E. Vine, a marginal note in the *Authorized Version* defines "authority" as an "eminent place."[5]

A cab driver can hold an eminent place within his realm of authority — the cab and the people in the cab. Too many times, we have taken this Scripture and applied it only to

---

[5]Vine, p. 89.

a small group of people when God meant for it to apply to a much larger group of people.

It applys not only to those in a place of high authority but also to those with an eminent place, an important place. Whether you know it or not, ushers have an eminent place in the church. They have authority. Who gave it to them? Their pastors did.

Let me give you an illustration. My staff and I were scheduled to go on a retreat. At this particular hotel, the meals had never been very good. When the secretary set it up, they wanted to serve cokes and coffee when we arrived. She told them not to do that and asked that they serve them after dinner. Well, they didn't pay any attention to her instructions.

We checked into the hotel in the afternoon and were relaxing. When it was almost time to eat, we cleaned up and went to the meeting room. I walked in there, and there wasn't any meal. There was only one waiter in the hotel, and he was doing room service. We were looking around for the meal, but it wasn't there.

My first thought was, "I'm paying the bill here. I will see that they straighten this out. If I don't get satisfaction with the catering people, I'm going to the manager. If he doesn't like it, I'll go to the owner of this place. If I have to, I'll go to the headquarters that runs this chain."

Now, there are times when we have rights. I am one of those people who tries to be sweet, but some people are just sweet by nature. My wife is one of those sweet people. I have to work at it. I am a mover and a shaker. If it doesn't look like it will work, I will make it work.

Many times as Christians we have misunderstood our rights and have rolled over and played dead when we should have stood up. Then there are times we stood up that we should have laid down. It takes wisdom to know when to do what. Right then, I was on my high horse and was ready to straighten some folks out.

Then the Spirit of the Lord said, "Why don't you practice what you preach?" Immediately, I began to follow the order of prayer I had learned.

Our people are free and easy, so they were serving themselves the coffee and water. Those were the only items in the room. Now remember, the waiter is doing room service too. He was all uptight and came running in saying, "If you'll put that down, I'll wait on you. Just wait!" He was all bent out of shape and frustrated. We were just trying to have something to drink while we were waiting. The tension was building in him.

The Spirit of the Lord said to me, "Befriend the waiter." So I started cutting up with him and getting him to laugh. What did I do then? I prayed for the catering man. Then I prayed for the cook and for the waiter. Why was I praying for these men when I wanted a meal? Because they were the ones with the food! Who had the authority? The catering man had the authority. He was the one who said to fix the food.

I could have stood there and said, "Father, I thank You that according to Mark 11:24, I believe I receive my food." I could have kept confessing and confessing, but I would have been misapplying the Scripture. When we do that, we get mad at God because He hasn't answered our prayer.

In this instance, I needed to be praying for men. When I prayed for men, the food was served faster than anytime I could remember, and it was the best we had ever had there. It was amazing. It startled me. Who did Jesus die for? He died for people, yet many times we spend all our time praying for things. I am not against praying for things, but why not spend our time praying for the people who have the authority over those things?

A Quiet and Peaceable Life

The result of praying according to the order of First Timothy 2:1 can be found in verse 2 . . . **a quiet and peaceable life.** Do you want to live a quiet and peaceable life? Things would not have been quiet and peaceable at the hotel if I had raised my voice and demanded my rights. But when I prayed according to First Timothy 2:1, I had a quiet and peaceable life.

After I had befriended the waiter, I went up to him at the end of the meal and put my arm around him and said, "You sure have been a blessing to us. I want to pray with you." He said, "No, I have to do room service, so I have to go!" He was nervous. The next day when I saw him, he said, "Hey, how are you Mr. Harrison?" He was open to me, and I could witness to him. If I had demanded my rights the night before, I couldn't have witnessed to him.

Look at verses 3 and 4: **For this is good and acceptable in the sight of God our Saviour.** Why? Because He **will have all men to be saved.** When we are living a quiet and peaceable life, it is easier for us to reach out to others and for them to receive what we have. He wants them saved from the wrath of men, saved from sin and saved from circumstances. What do they need to know? **There is one God, and one mediator between God and men, the man Christ Jesus; Who gave himself a ransom for all, to be testified in due time** (1 Tim. 2:5,6).

Just as the healing process can be sped up, so can people's salvation. How is the healing process sped up? When everything is kept right. When the wound is cleaned out and bandaged up properly, it can heal up much quicker because it doesn't have to fight infection. So it is with people's salvation. When they haven't been abused and battered by Christians, their due time can come sooner. Many times God has to work around His people and the

48

damaging words they have spoken. They get out there and make such a mess. It would help them if they would slow down and pray for people.

Many times Brother Hagin has said, "It's better to be too slow than too fast." I went to the Lord to find the truth in what Brother Hagin was saying. I wanted to understand. The Lord said, "It's better to be too slow than too fast because it's easier to play catch up than clean up." That is why many people aren't in the kingdom today. Some Christians are too quick with their temper. They say the wrong thing to people and make such a mess. Sometimes it takes someone else to come in and love the people until they reach the due time of their salvation.

I am not criticizing, but I do think we have lacked knowledge and haven't done things in order. If we will put it in order, it will work. It will be pleasing to God and will speed up people's salvation.

At one time, my personal life and ministry came under attack for things from the past. The past is the past. It is over. But some people try to be spiritual sheriffs. They are going to clean everything up and straighten everyone out. I have news for them. Only the blood of Jesus can do that!

When I came under attack, my first thought was, "God, strike him dead." Immediately inside, I knew I didn't get that from God because God is a God of love. He said, **. . . Vengeance is mine; I will repay (Rom. 12:19).**

What is my job? My job is to pray for them. Jesus in His Sermon on the Mount admonishes us to pray for those who despitefully use us and persecute us. (Matt. 5:44.) So I did. I took off time to pray and fast and find the Scriptures that dealt with this particular situation.

In the meantime, I was being mutilated, butchered and crucified. It is awfully hard to keep your mouth shut and pray the most effective prayer. I wouldn't pray in rage and anger. Fear tried to flood me. I thought, "I won't be able to preach again." But I searched the Scriptures, stayed in the Word and prayed in the Holy Ghost.

My ministry was under attack because of my past. People were saying things. Fear tried to grip me and say that my ministry would be destroyed, and I would never amount to anything. Fear said, "This is the end. Call it quits."

It took ten days of fasting and prayer before I could have the heart and mind of Christ. It took me that long to get myself purged and cleansed. During that time, I wrote out a petition. This was the first time I had written out a petition dealing in the area of relationships. I had petitioned the Lord in some less critical situations, but this was the first time I was dealing with something that was damaging to my heart, mind and ministry.

After considering wise counsel, I wrote out my supplication and made it just as legal as I could. My supplication was a little over two pages. Every time I made a statement, I wrote the Scripture reference in the margin. Out to the side, I had thirty-four Scripture references, plus eight in the supplication. So, I had forty-two references in all.

At the end of ten days, I had a prayer that I could pray. I prayed that prayer for that individual and two other people. One week later, all the evil communication from these three had dried up. The storm blew over. Why? Because God won't deny His Word. Prayer is the better way.

The normal reaction is to talk about them, fight, argue and criticize. The Church has resorted to the world's ways for years. God is ready to bring us in line with His truth and have us praying for those who would despitefully use us and speak evil of us. (Matt. 5:44.) In the process, we will start loving them and have nothing but the utmost respect and esteem for them.

Only God can put that in you. You can't manufacture it on your own no matter how good it may sound. When it isn't there, it isn't there. If God doesn't create the love inside of you by His Word and Spirit, it is all vanity and your efforts are futile.

But I can say I am walking in freedom today because I am in love with them. I don't have anything bad to say about them. I have nothing but good words to speak. I am praying for them, and the situation has turned around. It died a quick death. Why? Because I was praying the truth of God's Word. It is nothing I have done. It is not because I am a greater individual. It is all in God, in His Word, in His Spirit, and by the power of His name. I can be on top and shout the victory. I have no condemnation. I can go on and affect the lives God wants me to affect.

Knowing Him

The Bible says you will know the truth, and the truth will make you free. (John 8:32.) It is knowing the truth that makes you free. Jesus makes you free, but this doesn't become a reality until you know Him.

Everybody has their own working relationship with God. And you can't box anyone in. But the key to what makes it real and valuable is if you will build that intimacy with God so you know Him. When you know His voice, you don't have to have the spectacular. Let him speak to you in the way that He always does.

But the only way you will get to know His voice is by spending time with Him and developing an intimate relationship. Take my wife and me, for example. I can be in Botswana, Australia or Japan, but when I call my wife, she knows my voice. She has heard it enough times that she knows who I am without me even telling her my name.

51

Most Christians know the voice of the flesh and the voice of fear. There are many voices out there, and they all have significance. But the real question is, do you know His voice? Do you know Him?

To some people, God is way up in the heavens. That is wonderful and magnificent, but He also happens to be right down here standing right beside me. He is my friend, and I have Him in my heart with my arms wrapped around Him.

A Word of Encouragement

You may be questioning me right now feeling overwhelmed by your problems and circumstances. You may be saying, "I can't do anything right. My life is a mess, and it will always be that way." But that is a lie out of the pit of hell, for with God, all things are possible, but you have to get into the Word and spend some time with your Heavenly Father. As you do this, He will minister to you.

Maybe you are finding yourself in one of those critical situations where there seems to be no way out, then the prayer of supplication is what you need to pray. First, sit down and write out your petition. Then search the Scriptures to make sure that your request is in line with His will for you. Include those Scriptures in your petition. As you do this, you will find that your faith is rising. Your hope will turn to faith as you come to know what God's Word has to say about your situation.

Your supplication has dealt with the known will of God. But since your knowledge is limited, you must give the Holy Spirit free reign to deal with the unknown elements that may be involved. To do this, you must pray in your prayer language using the prayer of intercession. Worship is one of the best ways that you can make the transition from the mental realm to the spiritual realm. As you have your mind and your heart focused on Him, He will begin to take a hold, together with you as you pray. Your prayer will be according to the will of your heavenly Father and will cover all that you didn't know to pray. When you finish, you will have prayed according to all that you knew and covered every base that you didn't know. You will know that you know that you know. No one and no circumstance will be able to persuade you otherwise.

When you finish, it will be easy to thank Him because you will know that you have the petition that you desired of Him, and in the process you will have come to know Him and His love for you in a greater measure. When you pray like this, you can't be defeated, and you will see situations that you thought were impossible become possible with God.

A Psalm of Praise

So lift up your countenance and rejoice with me in the psalm that the Lord has given me saying:

I'm so glad I'm free.
Satan has no hold on me
'cause I'm free, and I'm rejoicing ever more.
Bless God, I've walked through a brand new
    spiritual door,
a door of prayer, and a door of praise.
And I'm gonna' do it with my hands upraised
'cause the Spirit of God, He's quickening me.
He's flowing mightily and flowing free.

So I'm rejoicing, and I'm singing the song.
I'm gonna' do it all the day long
'cause the power of God is coming alive.
Yes, sir, I'm gonna' jive!
Some of you have been confused.
You've thought, ''By the world, I've been used.

53

How can I arise and sing?
I need the help of my glorious King.''

Well, arise and stand in this hour,
and he'll deliver you by his power.
As you begin to praise,
it will not be delayed
'cause the Spirit of God wants to work in you.
He wants to work in everyone of you.
So allow His power to arise so strong,
and you'll find the days will no longer be real
    dreadful and long.

But you'll arise with a freshness of heart,
and you'll realize then that the Spirit of God is not
    going to depart.
But He'll sustain you and keep you by His power
because you're about to enter into your finest hour,
the finest hour for the Church to sing,
the finest hour to worship the King,
the finest hour to overcome,
the finest hour because the victory is already won.

So rejoice and sing a brand new song
and do it all the day long.

Appendix

The sample petition we looked at in another chapter of this book was taken from the legal form below written by Wayne Mathis, a Christian attorney.

Wayne told me that the rules of civil procedure in the state where he practices law are based on the Federal Rules of Civil Procedure. He said:

". . . these rules pattern their objective after God's rules. At the time these rules were drawn, it was the intent of the rule makers to impose standards which followed God's standards in the application of the business of the judiciary. It was assumed that men were aware of God's method of fairness in the dispensation of justice.

"It is ironic that such changes have taken place in our society today that I am now using these same rules in an effort to get a comprehension of God's method of fairness. The rules have not changed. We are just looking at them from the other side."

In other words, the rules of civil procedure in our country were written based on God's standards! And just as the people petition the courts of justice, we can petition the courts of heaven.

You may want to refer to Wayne's more technical petition as an example when you are writing your own.

* * *

CAUSE NUMBER: _____

IN THE MATTER OF	) IN THE SUPREME COURT
_____	) OF THE UNIVERSE
(name)	)
ET, AL as PETITIONERS	)

PETITIONERS' ORIGINAL REQUEST

Now comes _____, hereinafter referenced as "Petitioners", and file this their written request for specific relief for the reasons hereinafter set forth, pursuant to the directions of the Tribunal hereof wherein we are directed to make petition; to-wit: EPHESIANS 6:17, et seq., wherein it states that we are to take ". . . the word of God: Praying always, with all prayer and supplication in the Spirit, and watching thereunto with all perseverance and supplication for all saints." While Petitioners acknowledge that pleadings before this Tribunal may be oral, it is Petitioners' intent and desire to set forth this their request in plain and concise language, articulating the uncompromising Word of God which forms the basis of their request.

COUNT I.
JURISDICTION AND AUTHORITY

Petitioners are properly before this Authority, and this Authority has jurisdiction to hear and rule upon this matter. Furthermore, Petitioners have capacity to bring this request, and Petitioners are entitled to the relief sought for the reasons herein set forth:

1. We are citizens of the Kingdom of God and thus make our petitions to our Lord, the righteous Judge [See 2 TIMOTHY 4:8], who has delivered us from the

power of darkness and translated us into the kingdom of his dear Son [See COLOSSIANS 1:13].

2. This Ruler has authority to rule in this matter by virtue of the authority granted him. Reference EXODUS 15:18. [See also HEBREWS 1:8 ''. . . Thy Throne, O God, is for ever and ever: a sceptre of righteousness is the sceptre of thy kingdom.'']

3. This Tribunal has stated that petitions brought before it in accordance with the express will of the Judge will be granted. [See 1 JOHN 5:14,15 ''And this is the confidence that we have in him, that, if we ask any thing according to his will, he heareth us: And if we know that he hear us, whatsoever we ask, we know that we have the petitions that we desired of him.'']

4. We have the right and authority to approach the bench (throne) of this Tribunal boldly to proclaim our petition. Reference HEBREWS 4:16.

5. We have the right to request that this Tribunal act on our behalf as we are in good standing (right standing) with the Tribunal, having met all conditions precedent which are necessary to appear in this Tribunal, which condition precedent is righteousness before a righteous judge.

ROMANS 14:17 ''For the kingdom of God is not meat and drink; but righteousness, and peace, and joy in the Holy Ghost.''

HEBREWS 1:8 ''. . . Thy throne, O God, is for ever and ever: a sceptre of righteousness is the sceptre of thy kingdom.''

2 TIMOTHY 4:8 ''Henceforth there is laid up for me a crown of righteousness, which the Lord, the righteous judge, shall give me at that day . . .''

ROMANS 10:10 "For with the heart man believeth unto righteousness; and with the mouth confession is made unto salvation."

COUNT II.
APPLICABLE BASIS OF TRIBUNAL'S DECISION

Petitioners hereby submit that this Tribunal is a Tribunal following the rule of *Stare Decisis* as to all decisions; that is to say that this Tribunal abides by, or adheres to, decided cases and furthermore it is the policy of this Tribunal to stand by precedent, and once the Tribunal has laid down a principle of law as applicable to a certain state of facts, it will adhere to that principle and apply it to all future cases, where the facts are substantially the same. [See JAMES 1:17 ". . . with whom is no variableness, neither shadow of turning."] Therefore, Petitioners submit this their request confident that this Tribunal will be consistent in its rulings; and that this Tribunal will rule the same for each and every Petitioner bringing the same or substantially similar request for relief. [See ROMANS 2:11 "For there is no respect of persons with God."]

COUNT III.
COUNSEL FOR PETITIONERS

Petitioners hereby advise this Tribunal that they are represented by Counsel, whose name is, among others, "Jesus Christ, the Righteous", who is our "advocate with the Father." [See 1 JOHN 2:1.] [See also ISAIAH 9:6 "For unto us a child is born, unto us a son is given: and the government shall be upon his shoulder: and his name shall be called Wonderful, Counsellor, The mighty God, The everlasting Father, The Prince of Peace."]

COUNT IV.
CHANGE OF REPRESENTATION BY COUNSEL

Petitioners advise and represent to this Tribunal that past counsel, Satan, has been dismissed and no longer represents Petitioners in any matter, and specifically Petitioners plead to this Tribunal that past counsel is without authority of any kind, basis, or origin, as pertains to Petitioners. [See JOHN 17:16 "They are not of the world, even as I am not of the world."] [See also COLOSSIANS 2:15.] This petition shall constitute full notice to opposing counsel of all matters appertaining to this request, and accordingly no further pleadings referencing this request for relief will be forthcoming from Petitioners nor shall any further pleadings be allowed from opposing counsel.

COUNT V.
ABILITY OF PETITIONERS TO ADDRESS THE TRIBUNAL

Petitioners hereby advise this Tribunal that they are thankful to have the right and the privilege to present their case before a righteous judge (who has done great things on behalf of Petitioners and all others seeking relief before this Tribunal) [See PSALM 136:1-26], and therefore Petitioners enter this court with thanksgiving and praise [See PSALM 100:4]. Petitioners further submit to this Tribunal that the High Court has directed all persons under its constituency to submit prayers and supplications with thanksgiving [See PHILIPPIANS 4:6], with which Petitioners hereby joyously comply.

See also Petitioners' requests previously granted in numerous areas, but Petitioners call specific attention to relief recently granted; to-wit:

Provision of _____

_____

(list example here)

in response to written petition, wherein all relief requested by Petitioners was granted in full.

COUNT VI.
BASIS FOR REQUEST FOR GRANT OF RELIEF

Petitioners base this claim for relief in contract, calling the Tribunal's attention to the terms of the agreement as established in the statutory code hereinafter referenced as the Old Covenant and established by the sworn testimony of the Chief Justice of the Supreme Court. [See HEBREWS 6:13 "For when God made promise to Abraham, because he could swear by no greater, he sware by himself."] This covenant is based on the statements recorded by the Court Reporter of the Supreme Court, the Holy Spirit, through Moses [See EXODUS 24:8 "And Moses took the blood, and sprinkled it on the people, and said, 'Behold the blood of the covenant, which the LORD hath made with you concerning all these words'"], and further recorded the concept in NEHEMIAH 9:38, wherein it was stated, "And because of all this we make a sure covenant, and write it; and our princes, Levites, and priests, seal unto it," thus establishing the precedent for reliance upon a sealed covenant. This covenant was subsequently modified and ratified, by and through the acts of the agent of the Tribunal, Jesus Christ, as signified through the official seal of the Supreme Court, which was His blood. [See HEBREWS 10:29 "Of how much sorer punishment, suppose ye, shall he be thought worthy, who hath trodden under foot the Son of God, and hath counted the blood of the covenant, wherewith he was sanctified, an unholy thing, and hath done despite unto the Spirit of grace?"] Therefore, the blood incontrovertibly verifies and establishes that documentation hereinafter referenced as the new covenant. [See HEBREWS 13:20 ". . . our Lord Jesus . . . through the blood of the everlasting covenant" and HEBREWS 12:24 ". . . Jesus the mediator of the new covenant, and to the blood of sprinkling. . . .''].

COUNT VII.
EVIDENTIARY MATTERS

Opposing counsel is hereby estopped (i.e. precluded) from denying the veracity of the above referenced agreement, its legitimate nature, or from introducing any testimony in regard thereto as opposing counsel is a liar and the truth is not in him. He is the father of all lies, and as such cannot, in any form or fashion, contradict the evidence introduced herein. [See JOHN 8:44 ''Ye are of your father the devil, . . . [who] abode not in the truth, because there is no truth in him. When he speaketh a lie, he speaketh of his own: for he is a liar, and the father of it.'']

COUNT VIII.
REQUESTED GRANT FOR RELIEF

Petitioners, having established (1) that they are properly before this Tribunal, (2) that they are entitled to the relief sought, and (3) that this Tribunal has the power and authority to implement any judgment, decree or order entered herein, hereby plea to this Tribunal that they be granted the following specific request for relief, based on the following: (Set out specific relief sought in this petition and scriptural support therefore here.)

_____

_____

_____

_____

_____

_____

_____

_____

COUNT IX.
OTHER PROCEDURAL MATTERS

Petitioners hereby further represent to this Tribunal the following matters for consideration:

1. A Plea in Abatement (temporarily stopping this proceeding) will not be filed, as Petitioners do not have this matter pending in any other Court, and Petitioners specifically submit to this Tribunal that Petitioners will not ask that this matter be abated or held in abeyance through actions of Petitioners in seeking any relief in any fashion other than through this Tribunal. Petitioners submit this matter to this Tribunal and this Tribunal only, and will not under any circumstances take this matter back for further consideration or handling. Petitioners hereby represent to this Tribunal that they have cast the care of this matter upon the Tribunal, fully committed to follow the charge of the Tribunal as set forth in PHILIPPIANS 4:6-8.

2. Opposing Counsel has no effective pleas or defenses to the matters sought out herein.

3. To the extent the pleadings contained herein are insufficient, our Counsellor will plead our case. Petitioners remind the Tribunal that according to ROMANS 8:26 "the Spirit also helpeth our infirmities: for we know not what we should pray for as we ought: but the Spirit itself maketh intercession for us with groanings which cannot be uttered."

4. Petitioners submit this petition representing to this Tribunal that they have forgiven all Third Parties, which representation is a condition precedent to the receipt of the relief requested herein. [See MARK 11:25 "And when ye stand

praying, forgive, if ye have ought against any: that your Father also which is in heaven may forgive you your trespasses.'']

5. Petitioners submit MATTHEW 18:19 as applicable to this petition inasmuch as two are agreeing on earth as touching anything; therefore it SHALL be done for them.

6. Petitioners hereby confidently submit that this request for relief must be granted by the Righteous Judge of this Tribunal, by way of SUMMARY JUDGE-MENT; that is to say that no further hearing is necessary upon the matter in that Petitioners (a) have met all requirements set forth in the Word for the grant of this petition; (b) that Petitioners' request is properly founded in that it is not for Petitioners' lusts; and finally (c) that it is for purposes of allowing Petitioners to abound to every good work; to-wit:

(a) 1 JOHN 5:14,15 ''And this is the confidence that we have in him, that, if we ask any thing according to his will, he heareth us: And if we know that he hear us, whatsoever we ask, we know that we have the petitions that we desired of him.''

(b) JAMES 4:2,3 ''. . . yet ye have not, because ye ask not. Ye ask, and receive not, because ye ask amiss, that ye may consume it upon your lusts.''

(c) 2 CORINTHIANS 9:6-11 ''But this I say, He which soweth sparingly shall reap also sparingly; and he which soweth bountifully shall reap also bountifully. Every man according as he purposeth in his heart, so let him give; not grudgingly, or of necessity: for God loveth a cheerful giver. And God is able to make all grace abound toward you; that ye, always having all sufficiency in all things, may abound to every good work: (As it is written, He hath dispersed abroad; he hath given to the poor: his righteousness remaineth for ever. Now he that ministereth seed to the sower both minister bread for your food, and multiply your seed sown, and increase the fruits of your righteousness;) Being enriched in every thing to all bountifulness, which causeth through us thanksgiving to God.''

PRAYER

Wherefore, Petitioners, having plead before this court those matters establishing their entitlement to the relief sought and having presented sufficient conclusive evidence to support the findings sought, hereby request this Tribunal to enter a SUMMARY JUDGEMENT which grants to Petitioners all relief sought, and for such other relief as this Tribunal shall find appropriate.

DATED THIS THE _____ DAY OF __ , 19_____.

PETITIONERS:

(name)	(name)
(name)	(name)
(name)	(name)

DECREE OF THE TRIBUNAL

WHEREAS, on the above referenced date, in the above referenced cause, this Tribunal has conducted a full hearing of all matters therein; and

WHEREAS, THIS TRIBUNAL does find the Petitioners herein to be entitled to a grant of the relief sought;

NOW THEREFORE IT IS ORDERED, ADJUDGED, AND DECREED, that Petitioners receive that relief sought in COUNT VIII above; and

BE IT FURTHER ORDERED, ADJUDGED, AND DECREED, that such relief sought is granted IMMEDIATELY, pursuant to Mark 11:23-25; and

BE IT FURTHER ORDERED, ADJUDGED, AND DECREED, that the agents of this Tribunal are directed to implement such findings IMMEDIATELY, pursuant to Psalms 103:20 ". . . his angles, that excel in strength, that do his commandments, hearkening unto the voice of his word" and Hebrews 1:14 that says angels are ". . . ministering spirits, sent forth to minister for them who shall be heirs of salvation."

AMEN. SO BE IT.

Books by Buddy Harrison

Understanding Authority for Effective Leadership

Getting in Position to Receive

Maintaining a Spirit-Filled Life

Just Do It

Count It All Joy
Eight Keys to Victory in
Times of Temptations, Tests, and Trials
Coauthored by Van Gale

The Force of Mercy
The Gift Before and Beyond Faith
Coauthored by Michael Landsman

Available from your local bookstore
or from:

HARRISON HOUSE
P. O. Box 35035
Tulsa, OK 74153

Buddy Harrison is a man walking after love with an apostolic vision for what God is doing today. He moves in the gifts of the Spirit with sensitivity and understanding. He is Founder and President of Faith Christian Fellowship International Church, Inc. and Harrison House, Inc. in Tulsa, Oklahoma. He has authored several books.

As a small boy, Buddy was healed of paralyzing polio. More than 25 years ago, he answered the call of God on his life. He is gifted vocally and began his ministry in music and the office of helps. He became Office Manager for Kenneth E. Hagin Ministries and for several years pioneered many areas as Administrator/Office Manager.

In November, 1977, the Lord instructed Buddy to start a family church, a Bible teaching center and a world outreach in Tulsa, Oklahoma. He has obeyed the Spirit of God whatever the cost. Through his obedience, Faith Christian Fellowship was born with 165 people in January, 1978. Now there are more than 373 FCF churches worldwide.

Buddy and his wife, Pat, are known around the world for their anointed teachings from the Word of God, and for their ability to communicate principles from the Word with a New Testament love. Buddy attributes any success he has to obeying the Spirit of God and living the Word.

While in Israel, the Lord spoke to him to serve as pastor to pastors and ministers. His goal is to aid ministers in the spiritual and in the natural. Ministers around the world have received blessings through Buddy's apostolic ministry since he obeyed the vision given in Israel. Under his direction, FCF has grown to become a lighthouse for other Word and Faith churches. Today over 1,250 ministers are affiliated/associated or licensed/ordained through FCF.

For a list of cassette tapes
by Buddy Harrison
or for other information, write:

Buddy Harrison
P. O. Box 25443
Tulsa, OK 74153

*Please include your prayer requests and comments
when you write.*

In Canada contact:

Word Alive
P. O. Box 284
Niverville, Manitoba
CANADA ROA 1EO

For international sales in Europe,
contact:

Harrison House Europe
Belruptstrasse 42 A
A - 6900 Bregenz
AUSTRIA

The Harrison House Vision

Proclaiming the truth and the power
Of the Gospel of Jesus Christ
With excellence;

Challenging Christians to
Live victoriously,
Grow spiritually,
Know God intimately.